SAINTS AT PRAYER

A course on praying effectively in groups

LINK–WORK BOOK

Michael Mitton

LYNX
COMMUNICATIONS

Anglican
Renewal
Ministries

AUTHOR'S THANKS

I would like to thank the following churches for taking part in piloting this course:

All Saints Church, Woodbridge, Virginia, USA

St Alkmunds Church, Derby, UK

Bowthorpe Community Church, Bowthorpe, Norwich, UK

Church of the Transfiguration, Evergreen, Colorado, USA

St Mark's Church, Grenoside, Sheffield, UK

St Martha's Broxtowe, Nottingham, UK

Red Hill Christian Centre, Stratford on Avon, UK

My thanks also to those from the National Service Committee of Catholic Charismatic Renewal who studied the course and offered comments.

CONTENTS

INTRODUCTION
7   About this course

SESSION 1
The Father in heaven
11   Teaching points
12   Daily readings and prayers
15   Prayer idea

SESSION 2
The kingdom perspective
17   Teaching point
18   Daily readings and prayers
21   Prayer idea

SESSION 3
Presenting our needs
23   Teaching points
29   Daily readings and prayers
33   Prayer idea

SESSION 4
Repentance and forgiveness
35   Teaching points
37   Daily readings and prayers
40   Prayer idea

SESSION 5
Temptation and battle
41   Teaching points
48   Daily readings and prayers
52   Prayer idea

SESSION 6
Taking prayer out
53   Teaching point

APPENDICES
57   Appendix One – The gift of speaking in tongues
59   Appendix Two – Sources

Published by:

Anglican Renewal Ministries
45 Friar Gate, Derby, DE1 1DA

in association with:

Lynx Communications
Sandy Lane West, Oxford, OX4 5HG

ISBN 0 7459 3168 5

First edition 1994

Acknowledgments

Scripture taken from the Holy Bible, New International Version. Copyright
© 1973,1978,1984 by International Bible Society. Used by permission of
Hodder and Stoughton Limited.

Page 11, The Lord's Prayer; page 24, Intercession; page 35, Forgiveness:
quotations taken from *Prayer* by Richard Foster, reproduced by permission of
Hodder and Stoughton in UK and Zondervan/Harper Collins in the USA.

Page 20, *Link-Work Day 6*, Prayer: reproduced with permission from the
Episcopal Church of the USA.

Page 29, *Link-Work Day 1*, Prayer: taken from *By Stony Paths* by Jim Cotter,
Cairns Publications, 1991. Reproduced by permission of the publisher.

Page 37, *Link-Work Day 1*, Prayer; page 48, *Link-Work Day 1*, Prayer: taken
from *Celebrating Common Prayer* by Mowbray, 1992. Reproduced by
permission of the publisher.

Page 40, *Link-Work Day 6*, Prayer: taken from *Iona Community Worship
Book* by Wild Goose Publications, 1991. Reproduced by permission of the
publisher.

Page 42, Christian tradition: quotation taken from *Celtic Fire* by Robert Van
de Weyer, published and copyright © 1990 by Darton, Longman and Todd,
and used by permission of the publisher.

Page 50, *Link-Work Day 4*, Prayer: taken from *The Edge of Glory* by David
Adam, Triangle, 1985. Reproduced by permission of the publisher.

A catalogue record for this book is available from the British Library

Designed by: Wingfinger Graphics, 15 Queen Square, Leeds, LS2 8AJ

Printed and bound in Great Britain by Coventry Printers

Many believe that we are living at one of the most extraordinary and exciting moments in history. In many parts of the world we are seeing society under strain socially, economically and politically.

Graphic scenes of war, violence, famine, disease and pollution are constantly before us on the TV screens in our living rooms. As we approach the end of the twentieth century there is much to concern us about our wounded world.

Yet at the same time there is a stirring going on among God's people. Right across the world there seems to be a new clarion call going out from the portals of heaven, which is a calling to prayer. There has never been such a widespread desire among Christians to pray. Whether it be expressed in a praise march on the streets, or contemplative prayer in a side chapel, there can be no doubt that the Spirit of God is urging the church into places of deeper and sustained intercession. It is one highly effective response to a wounded and lost world. Only God knows what harvest this will reap, but we have every cause to have great expectations of our God of all hope.

It is with this in mind that I have written this course. The course is for any who feel that prompting of the Spirit to deepen their prayer life, in particular their prayer in groups. It is my conviction that some of the most effective prayer takes place when God's people come together. It is significant that the church of the Acts of the Apostles never seemed to be far away from a prayer meeting. But many Christians feel awkward and strangers in prayer meetings. I hope very much this course will help those who follow it to feel more at home praying in a group, and discover they have much to contribute to it.

The course has two component parts:

❖ The *Group Meetings* – of which there are six, structured on the Lord's Prayer;

❖ The *Link-Work Book* – provides daily readings and prayers for personal use for all who do the course.

It is my prayer that all who do this course will experience an awakening to prayer, both personally and in their group, thus joining in the fellowship of millions around the world who are being called afresh to pray.

Michael Mitton

INTRODUCTION

During the next five weeks you will be taking part in the *Saints at Prayer* course. At the group meetings you will be learning about prayer and praying together as a group. Alongside these weekly meetings you are invited to spend about fifteen minutes a day on your own for Bible study and prayer. These studies start immediately after the first meeting, and the last one is just before the final meeting.

The studies are designed for you to do on your own, but if you would find it easier to meet with a friend and study together, then please do.

You can do this study any time of the day. Make sure you have completed day seven before the start of the next meeting.

There are two parts to this time:

❖ Bible reading

❖ Prayer.

Bible reading

Each day you will find a daily reading from the Bible. Some of these will be directly related to the previous meeting. As you will see from the plan below, there is a weekly pattern to these readings.

Prayer

Each day you will find some guidance about prayer which will be connected with the Bible reading. Sometimes a prayer will be written out for your use; other times you use your own words.

During the coming weeks you are invited to take on three prayer projects. During the first week you will be invited to make your choices about these. The natural thing to do is to choose subjects which you are interested in and have a concern for. The three prayer projects are as follows:

❖ Personal prayer need

❖ Local prayer need

❖ Global prayer need.

PERSONAL PRAYER NEED

Choose a need that you are personally involved in. Maybe it is a friend who is ill, a god-child or a neighbour who is not a believer.

LOCAL PRAYER NEED

Choose a need in your neighbourhood. You might like to focus on a school, hospital or old people's home. You could pray for any projects in which your church is involved in caring for people in your locality.

GLOBAL PRAYER NEED

Here you will want to take up some national or international concern. It may be something that is headline news at the moment, or an area of the world that has been forgotten, but is still in great need.

During the first week you will choose a prayer need in each category. You can then record it in the boxes below and stick with it throughout the next five weeks. You will be invited to pray for each of these once a week, but it is likely you will want to bring them into your prayers more frequently.

My *Personal prayer need* is...

_____

My *Local prayer need* is...

_____

My *Global prayer need* is...

_____

Link-Work daily pattern

Each week's readings and prayers will follow this pattern...

DAY ONE

Bible reading

A psalm – you may like to make this as a psalm for the week, using it regularly in your worship and prayer.

Prayer

Related to the psalm.

DAY TWO

Bible reading

A reading from the group meeting.

Prayer

Personal prayer need.

DAY THREE

Bible reading

A prayer from the Old Testament.

Prayer

Based on the reading.

DAY FOUR

Bible reading

A verse for meditation.

Prayer

Prayer based on the verse.

DAY FIVE

Bible reading

A prayer from the New Testament.

Prayer

Local prayer need.

DAY SIX

Bible reading

On the theme of the week.

Prayer

Global prayer need.

LINK-WORK

DAY SEVEN

Bible reading

On the theme of the coming group meeting.

Prayer

In preparation for the group meeting.

Prayer idea

At the end of each week there is a *prayer idea* for you to use in your home.

Other useful information

You might like to record here the names of those in your group so that you can regularly pray for them through this course:

_____

_____

_____

_____

_____

_____

_____

The course is based on the Lord's Prayer which is printed here for you to use regularly:

Our Father in heaven, hallowed be your name,
your kingdom come, your will be done on earth as in heaven.
Give us today our daily bread.
Forgive us our sins, as we forgive those who sin against us.
Lead us not into temptation, but deliver us from evil.
For the kingdom, the power and the glory are yours,
now and for ever... Amen.

*Our Father
in heaven,
hallowed be
your name*

The Father in heaven

TEACHING POINTS

The Lord's Prayer

'The Lord's Prayer' as it is known must be the most famous prayer
in the world. It is recorded by Matthew and Luke. In Matthew's
gospel it comes as part of that great package of Jesus' teaching
known as the Sermon on the Mount (Matthew 6:9–13). Prayer is
one of the three "acts of righteousness" mentioned in verse 1 of the
chapter, the other two being giving (6:2–4) and fasting (6:16–18).
Matthew was keen that we should see this prayer at the heart of this
great section of teaching. No doubt Jesus repeated his teaching on
prayer on a number of occasions.

In Luke's gospel (11:2–9), Jesus teaches about this prayer after he
himself has been praying (11:1). The disciples were so struck by
Jesus' prayer, that they asked him, *Lord teach us to pray.* Most
translations of the prayer in Matthew's gospel do not include the
doxology at the end – *for yours is the kingdom, the power and the
glory for ever… Amen.* This is not found in the early manuscripts,
but is present in later ones, and was adopted by the early church
and became a normal part of the Lord's Prayer.

Richard Foster writes about the Lord's Prayer…

*It is lifted up to God in every conceivable setting. It rises from the altars
of the great cathedrals and from obscure shanties in unknown places. It
is spoken both by children and by kings. It is prayed at weddings and
death-beds alike. The rich and the poor, the intelligent and the
illiterate, the simple and the wise – all speak this prayer… It is such a
complete prayer that it seems to reach all people at all times in all
places.*[1]

Discovering the Father

Although God is in heaven, the whole thrust of the Lord's prayer
and the passages from Romans (Romans 8:1–2; 15–17; 26–27) is
that God is a Father who is intimate with us. The word **Abba** is the
name an infant gives to his/her father. The modern equivalent
would be 'Daddy'. When we read the gospels, one of the first
things that strikes us is the deep, personal and intimate relationship

of Jesus and his Father. For the faithful Jew, who did not even dare mention the name of God, to hear Jesus speaking so intimately to him must have been quite shocking. And then, more shocking still, Jesus invites his disciples into this same intimacy.

For many of us, there is still a journey of discovery we need to make. We may have known God as a remote and even severe parent figure, but have yet to discover him as the tender Father. We are permitted to know him as a Father because of the work Jesus has done on the cross, and we are enabled to experience him as Father by the gift of the Holy Spirit.

Our life's experience of our own parenting or early experiences of God received in church (eg: a distant God who resides only in the east end of church) can make it very difficult to comprehend this. For some, (eg: those who have suffered abuse) talk of an intimate relationship with Father can evoke painful memories.

But God has provided us with the gift of the Holy Spirit who enables us to experience this intimacy with Father. Apart from the Romans passage, see also Galatians 4:6.

The same Spirit who makes us aware of Father, also helps us to pray to him, even when we feel weak.

DAILY READINGS AND PRAYERS

LINK-WORK

DAY ONE

Reading Psalm 27

Go back over the psalm, and become aware of which parts of this psalm are special for you today. Perhaps you can use some of the verses as your own prayer. Notice especially the verses that speak about the protecting strength of the Father (eg: 27:1 and 5), and others that speak about his tenderness and his beauty (eg: 27:4 and 10). Spend a few moments thanking him for being your Abba, Father.

Prayer

Father in heaven,
Thank you that you are my light in the darkness
and my salvation from fear.
Help me to know that I am safe in you, even when troubles come.
Thank you for the glimpses you give me of your beauty and glory,
and that one day I shall see you face to face... Amen.

LINK-WORK

DAY TWO

Reading Luke 11:1–4

Think about the first meeting, and the discussion you had about the Lord's Prayer. How did you find the meditation? What do you think it was about the way Jesus was praying that so impressed the disciples?

Prayer

Use today the Lord's Prayer (see page 10). Say it thoughtfully, line by line, pausing where a particular phrase seems meaningful for you.

Today you need to choose your *Personal prayer need*. Once you have decided, write it down on page 8. Pray now for this need and use what you have learned about God as Father for your prayers.

LINK-WORK

DAY THREE

Reading 2 Chronicles 20:1–19 Jehoshaphat's prayer

Jehoshaphat's response to the threat of attack was to pray. Read this prayer carefully. Notice particularly that Jehoshaphat's main concern is for God's name (ie: reputation). He is not afraid to say, "We don't know what to do". He puts his trust in God, "our eyes are upon you". This king is prepared to be humble in prayer before God, even when the prophet had assured him of victory.

Prayer

If in your own life, or in the life of someone you know, there is a place of confusion which says, "Lord, we don't know what to do", bring this before God today. Use your own words, but use what you have learned from Jehoshaphat's prayer.

LINK-WORK

DAY FOUR

Reading for meditation: Romans 8:15

Read this slowly and thoughtfully several times. Then make it personal:

For I have not received a spirit that enslaves me to fear, but I have received a Spirit that makes me aware that I am his child, and this Spirit helps me to say with confidence, Abba, Dad, Father.

Keep going over this until you feel the truth of it deep in your soul.

Prayer

Come Holy Spirit,
fill me now with a sure knowledge that I am a child of God.
Thank you Jesus that you have enabled me to be adopted as a child of
my Father in heaven.
Father in heaven, I dare to call you "Abba", "Dad".
In the name of the Father, the Son and the Holy Spirit I arise today as
a child of God. Alleluia! Amen.

LINK-WORK

DAY FIVE

Reading Luke 1:26–38 Mary's Prayer

The prayer in this passage comes in verse 38. Although strictly speaking it is addressed to Gabriel, it is in reality a prayer to God, and one of the most remarkable prayers ever prayed when you consider what was being asked of Mary. Mary's prayer is an unconditional "yes" to God, even when he asks the apparently impossible. Mary is so secure in the knowledge that she is a child of God, that she has the freedom to respond with the obedience of a servant. Spend a few moments thinking about this passage, and what it must have felt like for this young girl to pray, "I am the Lord's servant. May it all happen according to your word."

Prayer

Ask the Holy Spirit to bring to mind any areas of your life where you need to say, "Yes, Lord according to your will." Remembering the example of Mary, pray your own prayer of obedience.

You need to choose today your *Local prayer need.* Once you have decided, write it down on page 8. Spend some time in prayer today for this need.

LINK-WORK

DAY SIX

Reading Mark 14:32–41

Just before his arrest, Jesus spent some time in the Garden of Gethsemane. He often sought quiet places for prayer, sometimes in quite remote places (see Mark 1:35). This garden seems to have been a favourite place for Jesus, and here his prayer time is one of great testing. But notice, he still experiences his Father as Abba. We have been learning this week that in all circumstances we can come to God as our Abba, Father.

Prayer

Spend some time today reflecting on what you have learned during this past week, speaking to him about anything you are finding hard to grasp, thanking him for new discoveries.

Today you need to choose your *Global prayer need*. Write it down on page 8. If the situation you are praying for is being reported in the papers, cut out the relevant sections and keep them with this *Link-Work Book*, to help guide you in your prayers. Offer this need today to the Father of all creation. Allow the Holy Spirit to "groan" within you (Romans 8:26), that is to help you to feel how God feels about the hurts in his world.

LINK-WORK

DAY SEVEN

Reading Matthew 13:31–33

Today you will be preparing for Session 2, which will be about the kingdom of God. Today's reading contains two parables about the kingdom that Jesus used. What do they tell you about the kingdom?

We shall also be thinking about how we listen to God and discern his will (*Your kingdom come; your will be done*). We shall be thinking about three important means of communication from God to us: the Bible, the gifts of the Spirit and creation. In preparation for this meeting, give some thought to how you have heard God speak to you.

Prayer

Pray for the coming meeting of your group. Pray for your leader(s), and pray for each of the people in your group. Ask God to breathe his Spirit on the meeting, particularly that you will grow in your ability to hear God.

PRAYER IDEA: PRAYER POT

Find a nice mug or pot and make it your 'prayer pot'. On little slips of paper write down names of people or situations that currently need your prayers. When someone asks you to pray for them, jot it down on one of these slips of paper. Have it handy for wherever you have your prayer time. If you have family prayers in your home, invite all members of the family to contribute to the prayer pot. When it comes to the prayer time, let God guide you as you shut your eyes and pull a slip of paper out of the pot and pray for that need.

*Your
kingdom
come, your
will be done
on earth as
in heaven*

SESSION 2
The kingdom perspective

TEACHING POINT

The kingdom of God

The teaching of the kingdom of God is at the heart of the Christian gospel, and formed a regular part of Jesus' teaching. Matthew prefers the use of the term, *the kingdom of heaven*, while Mark and Luke, writing to Gentile readers preferred *kingdom of God*. They both mean the same thing, namely the *kingly rule of God*. The Jews looked forward to that day when the kingdom would come – it was something the Messiah would usher in, so for John the Baptist and Jesus to say *the kingdom is at hand* was to say something truly momentous. They were saying, *It's happened – this is the moment we have all been waiting for – the great and mighty things of heaven are now come to earth.*

In Jesus' teaching, the kingdom has a present and future aspect. The present aspect manifests itself in all manner of ways in the person and deeds of Jesus. His teaching, healings, miracles and supremely his victory over sin and death demonstrated the presence of the kingdom of God on earth. This kingdom is a holy kingdom, and is of greater power than the kingdom of darkness which grips this world.

There is a future aspect as well. Although the kingdom is present in the here and now, it is only so in a provisional way. The kingdom still has a hidden aspect, like a seed in the ground. The king himself comes in disguise, as a servant. Those who know the kingdom now, also long for that day when the kingdom of God will be fully established in this world, when the devil, death and decay will be destroyed and the new heaven and new earth created.

To pray *Your kingdom come* therefore has two dimensions – there is prayer for the establishing of God's kingly rule in this world in the here and now, but there is also an expression of the future hope expressed in the New Testament prayer, *Maranatha, come, Lord Jesus!*

17

LINK-WORK

DAY ONE

Reading Psalm 19

Spend some time with this psalm. Note the close connection between God speaking through his creation (19:1–6, the sky, the sun) and through his written word (19:7–11, the laws and precepts). Spend some time today listening to God through his word, through aspects of his creation around you, and through the moving of the Holy Spirit.

Prayer

St Francis, as well as being a man of the Spirit and of the word, had a great love for creation. The following is a famous prayer of St Francis. You might like to use it, or adapt it to suit you:

So praise be you, my Lord, with all your creatures,
Especially Sir Brother Sun,
Who makes the day and enlightens us through you.
He is lovely and radiant and grand;
And he heralds you, his Most High Lord.
Praise be you, my Lord, through Sister Moon
And the stars.
You have hung them in heaven shining and precious and fair.
O praise and bless my Lord.
Thank him and serve him
Humbly but grandly!

LINK-WORK

DAY TWO

Reading Acts 2:14–18

God poured out his Spirit on the first Christians ten days after Jesus ascended into heaven, and he has been releasing his Spirit on his church ever since. Notice in this passage quoted from the prophet Joel that **all** are given ability to hear God and speak forth what they hear: sons, daughters, men, women, young, old, servants. Spend some time today breathing in God's Holy Spirit, asking him to open your eyes and ears to his voice.

Prayer

Focus your prayer today on the *Personal prayer need*. Before you start praying, give time to listening to God for that particular need. God may well be wanting to show you some specific area of need that it is right for you to be offering in prayer today. He may also want to speak to you about action you can take as part of the answer to your own prayer.

LINK-WORK

DAY THREE

Reading: 1 Kings 18:36–45 Elijah's prayer

This Mount Carmel contest is one of the most famous stories in the Bible. But look closely today at how Elijah prays. Elijah is not interested simply in people being entertained by the miraculous. His longing is for people to be so moved by God working in power that their hearts will be turned back again to him. Notice how he prays in verse 42 – he bends down on the ground and puts his face between his knees. Try doing this: it's not easy! It is a sign of utter beseeching. In humility, but also with confidence, he persistently prays for rain, until the dark clouds come with the promise of rain. Elijah is not afraid to be desperate and persistent in prayer.

Prayer

Allow God's Spirit to speak to you about an urgent matter for prayer. What is desperately needed in your life, in the life of a friend, in your church, your community or nation today? If you are feeling agile, then kneel before God as Elijah did, with your head between your knees and feel the intensity of this expressive position for prayer. If you are unable to adopt this position, find another that suits you, but which speaks of urgent prayer. Now let the Spirit intercede through you for this need. If you have the time, persevere until you sense you have completed this particular prayer task.

LINK-WORK

DAY FOUR

Reading for meditation: Matthew 13:33

Read this several times and allow the Holy Spirit to speak to you through this image of the yeast and the dough. How can the kingdom of God be mixed into your world today?

Prayer

Choose two or three people or situations you would like to pray for. Then, one by one, spend a few moments on each praying in this way:

Stretch out your hand over the person or situation as if they were there with you. Then pray, slowly and thoughtfully,

Lord your kingdom come on.
Your will be done (in his/her life/in this situation)

Be disciplined by using only these words, repeating them several times, and all the while imagining God working his kingdom work in this person's life/situation like yeast in the dough. See hope rising in the despair, health rising in the sickness, life rising in death etc.

LINK-WORK

DAY FIVE

Reading Luke 2:25–35 Simeon's prayer

Simeon is a natural contemplative and a man of the Spirit. He had spent many years devoutly waiting for the fulfilment of a promise he had heard God give him some time before. Notice the three references to the activity of the Spirit in his life. Because he has spent time in prayer, he is able to be 'moved by the Spirit'. Because he has spent time in prayer, he has heard God and is able to prophesy to Mary and Joseph about Jesus and even give a poignant word for Mary. Spend time in stillness this morning in the 'temple courts' with God. What does he want to show you?

Prayer

Today you are praying about your *Local prayer need.* Before you pray, be still with God and see if he wants to reveal to you anything about your locality that will help you pray more accurately.

LINK-WORK

DAY SIX

Reading Luke 6:20–26

Reflect today on the social dimension of the kingdom. Luke tells us that Jesus looked at his disciples as he taught them about poverty, hunger, wealth etc. Imagine he is saying this personally to you today. He looks you in the eye, with perfect love. Allow him to challenge you about the poor, the hungry and the hurting in his world.

Prayer

Today you are bringing before God your *Global prayer needs.* You may like to use this prayer:

Heavenly Father, who made us in your image and redeemed us through Jesus your Son: look with compassion on the whole human family.

Take from us the arrogance and hatred which infect our hearts; break down the walls that separate us; and unite us in bonds of trust and understanding, that we may work together to accomplish your purposes on earth, for the glory of your name; through Jesus Christ our Lord... Amen.[2]

LINK-WORK

DAY SEVEN

Reading Genesis 18:16–33

In this story we have Abraham, the friend of God, pleading with God to save a few people in Sodom. We shall be discussing this story in the coming group meeting. Notice how Abraham is humble yet confident in God's presence (18:22–27).

Prayer

In the next group meeting you will be invited to read out a prayer you have written. In preparation for this meeting, therefore, spend a few moments now composing a prayer about one of the three *prayer needs* you are concentrating on (*Personal, Local* or *Global*). Please note, the point of this exercise is not to see who can write the most brilliant prayer! The exercise is to help you prepare your thoughts before the meeting. If you prefer not to write anything down, it will be fine to say a spontaneous prayer when you get there. The writing down may particularly help those who feel a bit anxious about praying out loud in a group. Use the prayer now, as well as in the group meeting.

PRAYER IDEA: PRAYER PHOTO ALBUM

If there are people you regularly pray for, form a prayer photo album. It's often easier to pray for someone when you see their face, rather than just their name. Alongside the photo, you can have a sheet of paper on which you can write Bible verses that you feel are particularly important for that person, to guide you in your prayer. Or you may come across particular written prayers and blessings that you want to insert next to their photo. As you listen to God for that person, you may feel him speaking to you about them, and you can write down prophetic insight here as well.

SESSION 3
Presenting our needs

TEACHING POINTS

The Example of Abraham

The extraordinary story of Abraham and Sodom in Genesis 18:16–33, gives us an important insight into prayer.

Sodom was a city that had done terrible things and was so evil that God planned to destroy it. He decides to tell Abraham his plans. Abraham is upset by this, and enters into a dialogue with God which has a clear bargaining scenario about it.

Anyone who has been to the Middle East will be very familiar with the bargaining and negotiation that has to go on in order to buy something. This story has the same feel about it, and it seems almost outrageous to imagine little Abraham bargaining with almighty God.

Yet the story clearly shows that God is willing to listen. He listens because Abraham is the friend of God (James 2:23), and as such is able to enter into this negotiation, not in fear and trepidation, but as a trusted friend. Because Abraham is God's friend, God greatly respects him, so much so that he actually convenes the heavenly council at his tent (see the beginning of the chapter – the three visitors are part of the heavenly council). He tells Abraham his plans, but not only that, he gives Abraham the opportunity to speak in the court and speak in defence of the righteous people of Sodom and Gomorrah. Notice how Abraham is humble yet confident in God's presence (Genesis 18:22–27).

The point of this time of intercession is that Abraham is appealing for God to spare Lot and his family from the impending judgement on Sodom. God is clearly pleased with Abraham, for in Genesis 19:29, we read… *So when God destroyed the cities of the plain, he remembered Abraham, and he brought Lot out of the catastrophe that overthrew the cities where Lot had lived.*

Intercession

Intercession is a priestly* ministry. Moses is an excellent model of the priestly intercessor when he prayed for the Israelites battling against the Amelekites (Exodus 17:8–13). While Joshua engaged in the battle in the valley, Moses was up in the hills doing battle in the heavenlies in prayer. Interestingly it was Moses who became weary, which indicates he had the harder battle.

But the supreme intercessor in the Bible is our Lord Jesus *who died – more than that, who was raised to life – who is at the right hand of God and who also intercedes for us* (Romans 8:34). The writer to the Hebrews calls Jesus the great High Priest who *always lives to intercede for them* (Hebrews 7:25). The risen exalted Jesus is in the throne room of God right now making intercession for this world. He is continuing what he started in John 17 which is what we have noted before, the great High Priestly prayer.

By ourselves we have no entrée to the court of heaven. It would be like ants speaking to humans. We need an interpreter, an intermediary, a go-between. This is what Jesus Christ does for us in his role as eternal Intercessor… He opens the door and grants us access into the heavenlies. Even more: he straightens out and cleanses our feeble, misguided intercessions and makes them acceptable before a holy God. Even more still: his prayers sustain our desires to pray, urging us on and giving us hope of being heard. Richard Foster[9]

To **intercede** means to *stand between*. The supreme act of intercession was on the cross when Jesus stood between us in our sinfulness and God in his holiness. It cost him his life. Intercession always has a close connection with the cross and indeed with the resurrection. We come to God with the wounds of this sinful world, and we look to a God who both weeps for this world understanding its wounds, as well as bringing hope of resurrection.

The prayer jigsaw

The prayer jigsaw illustrates eight important aspects of intercessory prayer. They are as follows…

LISTENING TO THE HEART OF GOD

This is an essential part of the intercession time. Rather than coming to the prayer time with our agendas of our own concerns, we want to be open to hearing God for his concerns which may or may not coincide with ours. This will mean in practice having a

*THE WORD **PRIESTLY** IS UNDERSTOOD HERE IN ITS WIDER CONTEXT (SEE 1 PETER 2:5) AND IS NOT REFERRING TO THE DISTINCTIVE OFFICE OF PRIEST AS EXISTS IN SOME CHURCHES.

time of stillness at the start of the prayer meeting, opening our hearts to the Spirit of God. A time of worship is a very useful preparation for this, as we focus not on the needs of the world, but on God. We will need to hear what the will of God is for this particular situation so that we can pray not according to our wills, but to God's.

Example: In the time of waiting on God, three of the group have a strong sense that God is calling the group to pray for the unemployed of the area. As you wait on God, you feel his heart yearning for those who are suffering in this way.

USE IMAGINATION

As we come to pray, ask God to help by releasing prophetic and visionary gifts to us to help us imagine effectively the situations for which we are praying. The writer to the Hebrews encourages us to pray for those in prison *as if you were their fellow prisoners*, and those who are being ill treated *as if you yourselves were suffering* (Hebrews 13:3). This suggests entering into their world in our imagination. As we open ourselves in this way we may well find that the Holy Spirit gives a searching insight into a particular situation. This may have a prophetic dimension, as God reveals actual situations that require prayer.

Example: As you start to intercede, you see a picture in your mind of a Job Centre, and you see the expressions of hopelessness on the faces of people who are searching for work. Someone else sees a family under great pressure because both parents are unable to find work. Someone else is given the name of someone who is feeling very desperate.

PRAYING WITH THE SPIRIT

Any of the spiritual gifts can be used in prayer. We have already seen that the prophetic gifts are useful. In particular, the gift of speaking in tongues is very helpful in intercessory prayer. To help you with this, please refer to Appendix 1.

In Romans 8:26–27 we read… *The Spirit helps us in our weakness. We do not know what we ought to pray for, but the Spirit himself intercedes for us with groans that words cannot express. And he who searches our hearts knows the mind of the Spirit, because the Spirit intercedes for the saints in accordance with God's will.*

This is not an easy passage! But what is clear from the passage is that the Holy Spirit has a vital part to play in intercession and he is able to pray in and through us when we don't know what precisely to pray for. Praying in tongues is an excellent form of intercession because we become a very ready vehicle for the Spirit's prayers in which we are not encumbered by the need to find the right words, grammar etc, neither are we limited by our own minds. The other advantage, as we shall see in Session 5, is that speaking in tongues is particularly useful in spiritual warfare intercession.

In the context of the intercessory group, tongues is best used by all who speak in tongues, praying together. If only one person speaks in tongues then we are required to pray for an interpretation (1 Corinthians 14:13).

Example: As the group starts praying for the unemployed, those who use the gift of tongues feel moved to pray in that way. For about five minutes, there is united praying in tongues, following which there is a strong sense of the closeness of God and a new release of prophetic insight into the needs about which we are praying.

PRAYING WITH THE MIND

God expects us to use our intelligence when we pray! (By intelligence here, we mean our knowledge and understanding of a subject, not an ability to be or sound clever). This may be an obvious point, but it is one which needs to be made when groups get a bit 'super-spiritual'. Paul's teaching in 1 Corinthians 14:15 clearly says that praying in the spirit and praying with the mind have equal value, and both need to be used and neither should be denied or deemed inferior.

Example: During the prayer time, one member of the group who works at the unemployment benefit office speaks to the group for a few moments about their work, giving some helpful insight and making some specific suggestions for prayer.

PERSEVERANCE

The most frustrating prayer meetings you can go to are those ones where there is a 'prayer tour of the world' – when one person prays for the starving in Africa, the next person immediately prays for the situation in Eastern Europe, the next for the Brazilian rain forest and so on. When the Holy Spirit inspires us to intercession he will cause us to stick with one subject and persevere with that until there is a clear sense that the particular piece of intercession work is complete. There is short-term perseverance, which is to do with persevering with one prayer subject during a prayer meeting, and there is long-term perseverance, which is when God gives an individual or a prayer group a particular burden of prayer for a subject which may stay with them for months, even years.

Example: As the prayer meeting goes on it is clear that the unemployment issue is the main thing God is laying on the heart of the group to pray for. Rather than being distracted from this primary subject, members of the group are quite happy to keep praying about it for the whole meeting. Two of the group are given a long-term burden of prayer for the unemployed, and find it lasts for six months.

POSTURE

Sitting in what some have termed as the 'Protestant shampoo position' is not the ideal posture for intercession! Clearly people will have their own preferences, but the following points should be noted.

❖ The most comfortable position will probably be the least effective for intercession! Intercession is work, not relaxation.

❖ Sitting in an attentive way is well suited to listening to God.

❖ Standing is an excellent posture for intercession. It keeps you awake and alert, and is particularly helpful for authoritative prayer in spiritual warfare. Clearly standing can be tiring and people must be given the freedom to sit. Incidentally, why not try standing during the intercessions during Sunday worship - it can make quite a difference!

❖ Kneeling is appropriate for prayers of repentance and prayers of beseeching.

❖ Prostration is one stage on from kneeling. It is an act of humbling and is particularly appropriate when there is a strong awareness of the holiness of God.

❖ Hands and arms can be used in prayer. Upraised hands speak of receiving. Outstretched hands speak of blessing. If we will allow our emotions to be involved in our intercessions, then our arms and hands will express what we are feeling.

❖ Walking in prayer has been found to be very helpful, though it's not that easy for groups meeting in living rooms!

❖ Eyes – most find it easiest to intercede with their eyes closed, unless there is something helpful to focus on. However, please note that for someone new to group prayer there is something very strange about people meeting together, shutting their eyes and talking to an unseen God! You may need to explain it a bit.

Some people may find it helpful and inspiring to focus on a cross or some other visual aid that draws us into prayer.

Example: The group starts by standing, but it is not long before there is a strong sense of sorrow at the state of our society, and a number of the group feel moved to fall to their knees in repentance. One member feels this so strongly that he lies prostrate on the floor calling on God to have mercy on us as a nation for allowing so many to be unemployed. At one point the group feels moved to listen carefully to God and most sit. The group leader has placed on a table a cross and a candle as a visual encouragement to prayer.

SILENCE

There are two kinds of silence – the one which is very embarrassing because people cannot think of what to pray for or cannot express their prayer, so everyone becomes aware of their own inadequacy and the meeting is filled with a despairing sense of failure and weariness. This is clearly an unhelpful silence, and if you are leading such a silence, then it is better to put people out of their misery and bring the meeting to a close rather than sustaining discomfort. However, there is another sort of silence which is a very creative silence. This a silence in which the presence of God is very real, and it is an appropriate response to a holy God to remain quiet before him. This kind of silence is always under threat from those who are uncomfortable with silence, and the group leader will need to politely quieten any intruder, until (s)he feels that the time is right to start speaking again.

Example: Towards the end of the prayer time, there is a prolonged time of silence in which the group simply enjoys being in the presence of God. It lasts about five or six minutes. During this silence a number of the group feel that God has been giving assurance in the silence that he has heard their prayers.

BE YOURSELF

This does not need much explanation, but it is important to encourage people to be normal during a prayer meeting, and not to feel that they have to adopt particularly pious voices or religious jargon in prayer. Prayer jargon can be very irritating and seem unreal, and it is helpful if such language is politely and kindly challenged! We come to God in prayer with all our humanity. A part of this is that we may feel moved to express some deep feelings such as anger, joy, or sorrow. People should be encouraged to speak in their normal voice, rather than dropping it so low they cannot be heard. It is also sensitive for one person not to pray for too long. People sometimes get very anxious if they start praying at the same time as someone else. When this happens, do as you would in any normal conversation and say, *After you.* There is nothing unholy about doing the same in a prayer meeting.

Example: During the prayer time some of the group are in tears as they feel the pain of those without work. One or two feel a strong sense of anger in prayer as they feel indignant at what the enemy has done to God's creation.

DAILY READINGS AND PRAYERS

LINK-WORK

DAY ONE

Reading Psalm 59

This is an uncomfortable psalm to read. Notice the feelings that are stirred in this psalm. There is great indignation at the plight of the oppressed. As you consider before God today the hurting world around you, allow the Spirit of God to stir righteous indignation in you. These are feelings you can use creatively for your intercession.

Prayer

The following is an extract from Jim Cotter's prayer based on this psalm. Use it if you find it helpful (a **kraal** is an 'enclosure for cattle or sheep'):

Cruel men roam the streets in darkness,
howling like dogs, they prowl round the city.
They snarl and snap as they seize their prey,
they growl if their desire is frustrated.

I pray for the tortured and victims of malice,
for those imprisoned for no fault of their own.
My feelings run high – God forgive my excess –
why is your mercy and justice delayed?

Deliver the oppressed from the terrors of evil,
free them from those who relish their pain.
For the savage stir up violence against them,
waiting to knock at the door before dawn....

O God, from the depth of your love bearing pain,
break the cycle of our wraths and our sorrows.
For you are not a God who destroys,
you seek always to redeem and renew.

And so I will sing of your love and your power,
I will sing in the morning and tell of your goodness.

For you have been our strong tower,
a sure refuge in the day of distress.
I will sing your praise, O God my strength,
*for you are my kraal for ever.*⁰

LINK-WORK

DAY TWO

Reading Hebrews 7:23–28

Today, dwell on this thought of Jesus being the High Priest who prays for us. By ourselves we would have no rights to enter the court of heaven. We are separated by our sinfulness. But Jesus is the great High Priest, who welcomes us in by making us clean by his sacrifice on the cross. Not only does he allow us in, but he also he takes our feeble, often confused and awkward prayers and makes them acceptable before a holy God. And he prays for us, inspiring us to pray more and giving us confidence to know our prayers are heard.

Prayer

Spend some time thanking Jesus for being the perfect High Priest who was sacrificed for us. Thank him that he is now interceding for you, and not only that, he is offering your prayers before our holy God.

Now bring before him your *Personal prayer need.*

LINK-WORK

DAY THREE

Reading Isaiah 38:1–22 Hezekiah's prayer

Hezekiah became ill and was not surprisingly alarmed when Isaiah prophesied that he would not recover. But despite the prophet's pronouncement, Hezekiah cries out to God and perseveres in prayer. His prayer is recorded in verses 10ff. In response, God sent Isaiah back with the message that God would heal Hezekiah and give him another 15 years of life. Here is another example of God changing events because of prayer.

Spend some time reflecting on how persistent you are in prayer. You might like to look up the parable in Luke 18:1–8 about the persistent widow. Have there been times you have given up too soon? Can you resolve to become more persistent in prayer?

Prayer

Heavenly Father, forgive my faint-heartedness and the times I have given up too easily. Forgive me for the times when, like the disciples in Gethsemane, I slept when I should have been praying.
Send your Spirit upon me today to make me a worthy warrior in prayer, only ceasing when you give the word.
This I ask in the name of Jesus who persevered for me… Amen.

LINK-WORK

DAY FOUR

Reading for meditation Ephesians 6:18

Spend time with the various phrases of this verse which are full of meaning:

Pray in the Spirit...
on all occasions...
all kinds of prayers...
be alert...
keep on praying...
for all the saints...

Prayer

Lord Jesus Christ
take all my freedom,
my memory, my understanding, and my will.
All that I have and cherish, you have given me.
I surrender it all to be guided by your will.
Your grace and your love are wealth enough for me.
Give me these, Lord Jesus,
and I ask for nothing more.
Ignatius of Loyola (16th century)

LINK-WORK

DAY FIVE

Reading Acts 4:23–31
An early church prayer meeting

Peter and John have been warned by the Sanhedrin not to speak about Jesus (4:18). Persecution is threatened. The disciples' response is not to panic or fear, but to pray for boldness.

How does this prayer meeting compare to those you have been to?(!) What was it that made the Acts prayer meeting so vital and effective?

Prayer

According to your answer to the above question, pray that God would bless your group and stir you to pray with the same conviction and boldness as the disciples in Acts.

Pray today for your *Local prayer need*. Be aware of the Spirit moving in your heart, yearning for the needs in the people around you.

LINK-WORK

DAY SIX

Reading 1 Corinthians 14:1–20

The Corinthian church was definitely getting the gift of tongues out of proportion. But note, Paul does not forbid them from using the gift – he still encourages them. Public use of tongues needs interpretation, but we may use the gift privately without needing an interpreter. It is part of our work of praying in the Spirit. Praying in the Spirit is wider than just praying in tongues, but tongues can be a helpful part of inspired prayer. What do you think about this gift? If you don't have the gift, is there someone you know whom you can speak to about it? Perhaps you might like to ask God to give you the gift today, as you pray quietly with him. If you do use the gift, have you let it lapse?

Prayer

Pray today for your *Global prayer need*. If you use the gift of tongues, try spending about five minutes praying in tongues for this need. Notice, as you pray, how the Spirit stirs in you. You will not know exactly how you are praying for this need, but you may well become aware of the feelings of the Spirit moving in you. If you do not use the gift of tongues, pray in the Spirit nonetheless, asking the Holy Spirit to give you the words that are required for a time of persistent prayer. If you have the time, let this time of intercession run on until you feel you have completed your prayer task.

LINK-WORK

DAY SEVEN

Reading Matthew 18:21–35

The next group meeting will be on the theme of forgiveness, taking up the next phrase in the Lord's prayer. Use this parable to think about the theme. What is the main point of the story? What does it say to you?

Prayer

You might like to spend a few moments preparing for today's group meeting. There will be two exercises about forgiveness. In the first you will be invited to write on a slip of paper a 'sorry prayer'. It will be an opportunity to ask God to forgive you for your sins. Please be reassured, you are not being invited to drag out all kinds of embarrassing sins and talk about them in public! You can choose what you want to say sorry about, and you will be asked to share this with one other. Spend a few moments asking the Holy Spirit to search your heart for something that might be appropriate to share.

The second exercise is to do with forgiving those who have hurt us. As the parable shows, it is essential that we forgive those who have sinned against us. Clearly, where there has been very deep hurt, forgiveness may need to be done privately and in the context of inner healing. We suggest therefore that when it comes to the exercise, you don't select things which have caused deep hurt in your life. But in the normal course of events there are many apparently trivial hurts which come our way, and we need to freely forgive. Obviously the exercise is not designed for face to face forgiveness which is sometimes necessary. It will be focusing on heart forgiveness, where we forgive in our hearts those who have hurt us. It will heal any bad attitude we have to that person. With this in mind, spend a few moments in quiet and ask the Holy Spirit to alert you to any area of unforgiveness in your life at the moment that might be helpful to confess in the context of the coming group meeting. Please note, this exercise will be done privately and you won't be required to reveal any details to anyone.

There is no compulsion to do either of these exercises, but it is a great opportunity, so use them if you can.

PRAYER IDEA – THE PRAYER PLACE

People are increasingly finding it helpful to have a special place in the home set aside that can be a 'prayer place'. Even in the most congested of homes, it is possible to find an agreed corner somewhere in the house that can be acknowledged by the household as a prayer place. According to your spirituality, you can bring to this prayer place things that are meaningful to you – pictures, books, candles, a cross etc. Even if you have members of your household who are not committed Christians, they may well appreciate this quiet place, for most people want to pray from time to time. There should be an agreed rule that anyone can come to this prayer place at any time and be left in peace.

Forgive us our sins, as we forgive those who sin against us

SESSION 4
Repentance and forgiveness

TEACHING POINTS

Forgiveness

The concept of forgiveness is very easily misunderstood.

Richard Foster gives a very helpful guide to what forgiveness is and what it is not.[9] It includes the following points, which are essential to understand if we are to grasp the full meaning of forgiveness.

❖ Give comes before **forgive** in the Lord's Prayer – we cry out **forgive** in response to God's good gifts to us.

❖ This is the only petition Jesus amplifies (Matthew 6:14–15).

❖ He understood therefore that it would be difficult for us to get hold of this.

❖ Forgiveness does not mean that we will cease to hurt. Just because we still feel sore, does not mean we have failed to forgive.

❖ Forgiveness does not mean we will forget, but we do not use the memory to hurt others.

❖ Forgiveness does not imply that the offence did not really matter.

❖ Forgiveness does not mean acting as if things are just the same as before the offence.

❖ Forgiveness is a miracle of grace whereby the offence no longer separates us from the one who has hurt us.

❖ God has bound himself to forgive when we forgive. No matter how guilty we feel, when we forgive others, God freely forgives us.

C. S. Lewis points out that people often find it hard to forgive, because they think this means they are excusing the person. He writes…

There is all the difference in the world between forgiving and excusing. Forgiveness says, "Yes, you have done this thing, but I accept your apology, I will never hold it against you…". But excusing says, "I see that you couldn't help it, or didn't mean it, you weren't really to

35

blame." If one really was not to blame, then there is nothing to forgive. In that sense forgiveness and excusing are almost opposite.⁶

The Lord's Prayer was given for us to say corporately, and so the forgiveness as expressed in this prayer is corporate – *as we forgive those who have sinned against us.* There will be occasions then when it is appropriate for the community of Christians to express forgiveness together on behalf of the community.

Intercessory repentance

In 587BC, Jerusalem was razed to the ground by Nebuchadnezzar, and the Jews were taken into captivity in Babylon. Jeremiah had prophesied a 70-year period of captivity in Babylon, after which there would be a gradual return to Jerusalem. The great empire of Babylon collapsed, and the Assyrians who now dominated were far more tolerant of the Jews and allowed them to return, even to rebuild the temple. In the 5th century BC, two key figures emerged who were used by God to rebuild the city walls and encourage God's people, namely Ezra and Nehemiah, whose books can be found after 2 Chronicles in the Bible.

Both Ezra and Nehemiah were godly, humble men who were very aware of the sins of previous generations of God's people and were determined that the folly and faithlessness of days gone by should not be repeated. Ezra was clearly a great intercessor, and the prayer recorded in chapter 9 gives an insight into his prayer life. According to the Jewish law, Jews were not allowed to marry "foreigners". Experience in the past had shown that to do this led inevitably to idolatry. If God's people now started to break one of the major laws, then they would be repeating the same sins of their forefathers, and they would be in great trouble.

So in Ezra 9:5, he cries out to God in prayer about the problem. The important point to notice in this prayer is the word **we**. Ezra identifies with his people in prayer, so much so that he actually confesses on their behalf (eg: '**our** sins are higher than our heads... **our** guilt has been great... **we** have disregarded the commands you gave through your servants the prophets.') He is even willing to identify with previous generations. His repentance goes beyond himself, and beyond his own generation.

As Ezra prays and confesses in this way he becomes so deeply involved and moved by it, that in chapter 10 we see that others become involved and are convicted of sin. Almost immediately, Ezra's prayers are answered.

We are permitted to pray as Ezra did. Admittedly, Ezra was a priest and it was part of his priestly duty to pray. But in prayer we all have a priestly duty as we are part of the priesthood of all believers. We too are part of communities that have sinned, either recently or in the past. We too are part of communities that are in danger of breaking God's laws, and we urgently need to intercede on their behalf.

DAILY READINGS AND PRAYERS

LINK-WORK
DAY ONE

Reading Psalm 51

This is king David's famous prayer of confession after he had committed adultery with Bathsheba and effectively murdered her husband. Spend some time reflecting on this psalm, especially in the light of the exercises you did at the last group meeting.

Prayer

Use verse 10 as a repetitive prayer, saying it slowly several times giving time to become aware of God cleansing your heart and renewing your spirit.

You may like to use this prayer:

Take away, O Lord, the sin that corrupts us;
restore by grace your own image within us;
give us the sorrow that heals
and the joy that praises,
that we may take our place among your people,
*in Jesus Christ our Lord… Amen*❼

LINK-WORK
DAY TWO

Reading Romans 3:21–26

Paul loves the word 'justified' and uses it 22 times! Because of Jesus dying on the cross on our behalf, God declares us *not guilty*, and indeed he declares us righteous. It is "just if I'd" died on the cross, taking the penalty for sin.

Prayer

Spend some time today thanking the Lord Jesus for going to the cross for you and taking upon him the payment for your sin, and for giving you the gift of eternal life. If you have a cross or crucifix, take hold of it and ask God to give you a fresh insight into its meaning for you today.

Pray for your *Personal prayer need* today.

LINK-WORK

DAY THREE

Reading 1 Samuel 1:1–20 Hannah's prayer

Hannah's prayer is the prayer of desperation. As with all desperate prayers it is not wordy, but short and to the point. She is not afraid of crying out to God about her need. Notice the expressions used about her prayer (NIV): *In bitterness of soul Hannah wept much and prayed to the Lord* (verse 10); *Hannah was praying in her heart... Eli thought she was drunk* (verse 13); *I am a woman who is deeply troubled* (verse 15); *I was pouring out my soul before the Lord* (verse 15); *I have been praying here out of my deep anguish and grief* (verse 16). Hannah's pain is a pain of longing, but she directs this longing not to self pity or bitterness, but into heartfelt cries before God. Although her prayer is finally and gloriously answered, it is not before years of longing and hurtful ridicule from Peninnah (verses 6–7).

Prayer

Spend a few moments reflecting on Hannah's prayer. How do you pray when you feel desperate or hurt? Is there a longing in your heart that needs expression before God today? There may be others who you know who are longing for God to hear them. Pray for them today, taking Hannah's prayer into their situation.

When you have finished your prayer, read 1 Samuel 2:1–10, which is Hannah's prayer of praise and thanks following answered prayer.

LINK-WORK

DAY FOUR

Reading for meditation 1 John 1:8–9

Spend time meditating on this verse, allowing the truth of it to reach your heart.

Prayer

One person in the New Testament who felt terribly burdened with guilt was Peter after he had denied knowing his friend and master when he most needed him. Peter must have wondered whether Jesus could possibly forgive him, and whether he could use him again. But in John 21:15–18, Jesus demonstrates that he has not only forgiven Peter, but he reinstates him for the work of feeding his sheep.

After reading this story, try and 'get into' it by imagining the scene... You are beside the lakeside on a bright morning just after sunrise. The warmth of the sun is on your back, and its light is flickering on the water. On the shore is a little charcoal fire, and Jesus has been cooking some fish and bread. You have eaten from this meal, and you can see Jesus speaking with Peter as he forgives and restores him. You see them embracing, hugging each other.

Peter has tears running down his delighted face.

Then Jesus comes over to speak with you. Be aware of how it feels to be alone with the risen Jesus at this lakeside meeting. For you too have had your moments of denying Jesus and departing from his ways. You, like Peter, are aware of shame as Jesus draws close. But become aware of how he looks at you... Talk to him in these few moments, then wait and listen for his word to you... When you have heard, let Jesus embrace and hold you, giving you strength to go out, restored and renewed.

LINK-WORK

DAY FIVE

Reading Acts 9:10–19 Ananias' Prayer

Here we have an example of conversation prayer. Ananias, like Abraham, feels secure enough in the love of God to argue with him. Surely God can't be telling him to go and lay hands on the one man who is set on exterminating all Christians! Ananias was available for God to call him and use him. Following his time of hearing God, he went and prayed for Saul. What do you learn about prayer as you think about this story?

Prayer

Pray for your *Local prayer need* today. As you pray and listen to God, is he directing you to take any action today to be part of his answer to your prayers? Ananias may well have been praying about the situation of Saul coming to Damascus, when God called him to take action about it. Be open to God, even if he calls you to do something surprising!

LINK-WORK

DAY SIX

Reading Ezra 9:1–15

You looked at this passage in your group last week. Go over this passage again, looking at the way Ezra prays for his people. Notice how he is prepared to take responsibility in prayer and is willing to pray on behalf of his people.

Prayer

As you bring before God today your *Global prayer need*, consider if there is any way you can be engaging in intercessory repentance in connection with this. It may be on behalf of the church, or the nation or some other group which is responsible for injustice and suffering.

You may like to use this prayer from the Iona Community...

O God, gladly we live and move and have our being in you.
Yet always in the midst of this creation-glory,
We see sin's shadow and feel death's darkness:
Around us in the earth, sea and sky, the abuse of matter;
Beside us in the broken, the hungry and the poor,
The betrayal of one another;
And often, deep within us, a striving against your Spirit.
O Trinity of love,
Forgive us that we may forgive one another,
Heal us that we may be people of healing,
And renew us that we also may be makers of peace.[8]

LINK-WORK

DAY SEVEN

Reading Ephesians 6:10–20

In the coming group meeting we shall be thinking about the spiritual battle, and this passage from Paul's letter to the Ephesians alerts us to the reality of the battle, and the need to engage in it in prayer. As you prepare for the group meeting, spend a little time gathering together your own thoughts about spiritual warfare. Is it something you have been aware of in your own life? How do you understand these powers of darkness that Paul speaks of?

Prayer

As you prepare for the next meeting, ask God to direct your group leader(s), giving them wisdom as they lead the meeting. Pray for the other group members by name, asking specifically for God's protection on them.

PRAYER IDEA – PRAYER STONES

For your prayer place, you may find it helpful to collect stones and shells from special places. For example, if you travel or have friends who travel, bring back stones from that place so that you can be reminded to pray for that country. Take the stone in your hand as you pray for the people of that country. You could also collect stones from your neighbourhood – eg: from around your hospital, school etc and place them around a cross in your prayer place. You can also collect beautiful rocks, shells etc which simply speak of God's creation. At certain times of the year you can use these stones in other ways – for example during Holy Week you can form them into a cross; at Christmas you can use them as part of a crib etc.

SESSION 5
Temptation and battle

TEACHING POINTS

Temptation and testing

The word **tempt** suggests being led into evil. But the word Jesus uses in the prayer here is better translated *test*. When Jesus urges us to pray in this way, he is not suggesting that God might be inclined to lead us into evil ways. God would never seduce us into sin. But Jesus is suggesting that we will be tested. When we read of the temptations of Jesus in the wilderness, it begins, *Then Jesus was led by the Spirit into the desert to be tempted by the devil* (Matthew 4:1). The Holy Spirit clearly was not leading Jesus into sin. The understanding of tempting is to do with being tested, such that through the testing there is a growing in strength.

William Barclay puts it like this…

Temptation is not designed to make us fall. Temptation is designed to make us stronger and better men and women. Temptation is not designed to make us sinners. It is designed to make us good. We may fail the test, but we are not meant to. We are meant to emerge stronger and finer.[9]

This part of the Lord's Prayer is requesting that we will not be led into that tempting in which we fail. God may well lead us to times when we are tested in such a way that causes us to grow.

Jesus entered into this kind of testing when he entered the wilderness after his baptism in the river Jordan. The story is recounted in Matthew 4:1–11. At the end of a long period of fasting, the testing becomes acute as Satan is permitted to test Jesus in three key areas of life…

1   He was tempted to turn stones into bread. This was a temptation to put his physical needs before his calling to be obedient to his Father.

2   He was tempted to leap down from the pinnacle of the temple to see if God would rescue him. This is a temptation to control and manipulate God, as well as the temptation to test him out to see if he is trustworthy. It is quite contrary to the call to trust God completely, and to let him rule in our lives in his way.

3 He was tempted to seek worldly power and glory, which is contrary to the kingdom way of humility and giving glory to God.

NOTE

Jesus was not ashamed of the fact that he was tempted. He must have told others about it, else it would never have been recorded by the gospel writers. There is no shame in being tempted – only in giving in to temptation.

The reality of the battle

The Bible, Christian tradition and our experience all testify to the reality of the spiritual battle.

THE BIBLE

The fight is not against flesh and blood but against a spiritual foe. Ephesians 6:10–18

There is a war on and we are given spiritual weapons to use in the fight. 2 Corinthians 10:3–5

In Philippians 2:25 and Philemon 2, Paul uses the term 'fellow soldier' of his fellow Christians, indicating that to be a Christian is to be part of an army.

CHRISTIAN TRADITION

The first people to evangelise these isles believed very much in the reality of the spiritual battle. A great evangelist in Wales during the fifth century was Iltut. His life-long ambition was to be a soldier, especially after hearing of the bravery of King Arthur. He indeed became a soldier, but one day during a hunting expedition, he met a monk called Cadoc who lived alone in a forest. He was greatly convicted of sin and profoundly impressed by the life of Cadoc. That night he thought long and hard about the battles he had fought, and the spiritual battles this hermit was fighting in prayer. When he had fallen asleep, *an angel came and spoke to Iltut in a dream: "Until now you have been a knight serving mortal kings; from now on I want you to be a knight in the service of an immortal king, the King of all kings." At dawn the following morning Iltut crept out of the royal palace, leaving behind his sword and armour, and wearing only a rough woollen cloak. His heart was filled with both joy and fear, as he set out to join God's army he knew that the war against Satan is far harder than any human wars, but the rewards far greater."* ⓫

In the Anglican church when people are baptized, the minister will say the following baptismal prayer:

I sign you with the sign of the Cross, the sign of Christ. Do not be ashamed to confess the faith of Christ crucified; fight valiantly under the banner of Christ against sin, the world and the devil, and continue his faithful soldier and servant to the rest of your life.

May Almighty God deliver you from the powers of darkness, and lead you in the light and obedience of Christ.

OUR EXPERIENCE

Most Christians can testify to times in their life when they have felt the reality of the battle.

What is spiritual warfare?

Spiritual warfare is the battle for the kingdom of God.

The kingdom of God is the kingly rule of God. The kingdom of God, then, is when God is allowed to rule in this world, and manifests his rule through the power of the Holy Spirit and in the authority of his Son, Jesus, thus reversing the evil things Satan has done to this world, and bringing about all the good things of the kingdom.

SATAN

Satan was one of God's creatures, made originally good, but who became consumed by pride. Luke 10:18 and Revelation 12:7–9 indicate that he (or more accurately **it**) rebelled against God, fell from heaven and set up on earth in opposition to God. Because God created and loved this world, it was the obvious place for Satan to wage his warfare.

In Ephesians 6:12, Paul teaches that our struggle is against a range of spiritual powers (hierarchies, authorities and world controllers). The malevolent creatures in Satan's army are called **demons** in the Bible. They range in their power and influence, and some form a particular attachment with people. When this is the case the person is described in the Bible as being **demonized**. The term 'demon-possessed' is unhelpful, and it is more accurate to speak of people being afflicted by a demon. People who are demonized need the ministry of deliverance to free them.❶

JESUS AND THE SPIRITUAL BATTLE

Jesus came into this world as light into darkness, scattering the darkness of Satan.

The reason the Son of God appeared was to destroy the devil's works.
1 John 3:8

Immediately after the wilderness temptations, Jesus returns to Galilee in the power of the Spirit. From that point on he is constantly encountering the effects of Satan's work in this world (demonic oppression, sickness, death, hostility in nature, poverty, injustice etc.). He frequently has what John Wimber terms 'power encounters'. See, for example, how Mark describes the beginning of Jesus' ministry in Mark 1:21–34.

The great climax of this battle with Satan came at the cross. The cross is the supreme example of Jesus' trusting obedience, and it is the supreme humiliation of the enemy.

The cross represents a victory over Satan because…

❖ Jesus was totally obedient to God's will (Philippians 2:5–11), in contrast to Adam's disobedience in the garden of Eden.

❖ He took upon himself the sin of the world. Satan's plan was to keep the world bound in sin; Jesus has freed us by his sacrifice on the cross which has paid the price of our sin. (Isaiah 53:5)

❖ He inflicted a mortal wound on Satan and all his demons (Colossians 2:15)

In 1 Corinthians 15:20–26 Paul makes it abundantly clear that Jesus, having risen from the dead, has the power and authority over death. Death was introduced into the world by Satan. Jesus has rescued us from it.

NOTE

Verse 26 tells us that one day death itself will be destroyed once and for all. Hallelujah!

When Jesus returns he will destroy Satan and his demons and the world will be rid of Satan's influence.

See… Revelation 20:10 and 21:1–4

A German theologian, Oscar Cullman, has given a very useful analogy to describe the situation as it exists at the moment, between the cross and the ultimate destruction of Satan. He compares it with the situation that existed in the Second World War between D Day (6 June 1944) when it is generally reckoned victory was assured, and VE Day (8 May 1945) when victory was achieved. However those eleven months in between saw some of the heaviest fighting and the greatest loss of life. Although we fight a defeated foe, the battle can still be tough.

Spiritual warfare in the life of the church

Some idealists may see churches as wonderful fortresses of holy living, defended against the forces of the enemy by the ongoing life of worship and prayer. It would not occur to some people to see church as a battleground. However, in many people's experience, the church is very much the object of Satan's attacks, and far from being defended from such attacks, many churches find their spiritual lives and witnesses stifled by the effects of sin and Satan.

In the opening chapters of the book of Revelation, a number of churches are singled out for words of warning and encouragement from Jesus. Take note of the following…

Smyrna	the devil will put some of you in prison to test you…
Pergamum	I know where you live, where Satan has his throne…
Thyatira	You tolerate that woman Jezebel, who calls herself a prophetess. By her teaching she misleads my servants into sexual immorality…
Philadelphia	I will make those who are of the synagogue of Satan, who claim to be Jews though they are not, but are liars – I will make them come and fall down at your feet…

These young churches, despite being lively, powerful and charismatic were nonetheless vulnerable in the spiritual battle. The note of battle is very clear here, and Jesus warns about Satan's plans to frighten and persecute; he gives insight and information about the spiritual state of the city; he warns about specific individuals who are an influence for darkness; and he alerts them to whole groups of people who are being used by Satan to damage the church.

The church has traditionally recognized that the three categories of attack are…

❖ the world
❖ the flesh
❖ the devil.

Just as these can be areas of vulnerability for individuals, so can they be for churches. Thus...

THE WORLD

Jesus called Satan *the prince of this world* (John 12:31) and whilst the world has much good in it, it has been confused and its values distorted by the enemy. Worldliness creeps into church in all kinds of ways – in the way we handle our money, in our dealings with one another, how we treat visitors, our attitude to ethnic minorities etc. Unchristian values which are popular in the world can all too easily become acceptable in the church.

THE FLESH

This refers to the fallen human nature within us which expresses itself as sin. Personal sin inevitably has consequences for the community, and Satan will seek to undermine the work of God in churches by distracting people into sin. You sometimes find in churches patterns of sinful behaviour which go back for generations.

THE DEVIL

The devil is clearly active in the other two, though they can equally be the fault of our own rebelliousness and foolishness, and we have to learn to discern where responsibility lies. Whilst Satan will seek to use our weaknesses in the areas of the world and the flesh, he may also seek to undermine the work of the church through all kinds of counterfeit powers. There are a whole number of activities which open people to darkness (eg: spiritualism, astrology, explorations into psychic powers, New Age etc). Where people in the church are dabbling in these, the spiritual life of the church will be affected.

Helps for spiritual warfare

AUTHORITY

Psalm 8:6 and Genesis 1:26 – we were made to have authority over creation. We are part of a royal priesthood. In Mark 11:22–25, Jesus gives us permission to command things in the ways he did. This means that it is appropriate on some occasions to use a command prayer (For example: *in the name of Jesus we forbid all forces of darkness to send division to this church.*), rather than a request prayer (For example: *Lord, protect us from our enemy who seeks to send division to this church.*). This is really a very simple point, but very crucial in the spiritual battle. Many Christians have never taken up the authority God wants to give them in prayer. Such authority must of course be used responsibly and in such a way that God is glorified.

Note: Using your authority does not necessarily mean raising your voice!

PRAISE

Satan hates it when God is worshipped and praised. Songs and prayers of praise are an excellent way of preparing for spiritual warfare intercession. Acts 16:25 – we see Paul and Silas praising God in their prison cell. It was the praise that triggered their release.

THE WORD OF GOD

In the list of armour in Ephesians 6, the word of God is pictured as a sword of the Spirit, (verse 17) and it is the one offensive weapon. Jesus used this weapon most effectively in the battle in the wilderness (*It is written...*). Satan is the father of lies and hates truth. When confronted with the truth of God's word used in faith, he is on the run.

FASTING

Fasting is the forgotten prayer discipline, and is a tremendously powerful weapon in our spiritual armoury. Jesus expects his disciples to have a regular discipline of fasting (Matthew 6:16–18). On a practical note, there are many ways of fasting, but perhaps the most straightforward is to do a 24-hour food fast from supper one evening to supper the next.

SPEAKING IN TONGUES

This is a very useful gift in the spiritual battle and should be used by those who have the gift. In Ephesians 6:18, Paul ends his teaching on the armour of God with the exhortation to *pray in the Spirit on all occasions, with all kinds of prayers and requests* – this would certainly include prayer in tongues (see Appendix One). Only God understands tongues, which means they are unintelligible to Satan. It can also be an advantage that we don't understand them, as some aspects of the spiritual warfare are well beyond our understanding.

LINK-WORK

DAY ONE

Reading Psalm 18

Some people are uncomfortable with psalms like this, and indeed it would be offensive if we were to use it to support warring against people. But under the new covenant, we understand the warfare to be in the heavenlies. When used in this way, this psalm is a powerful weapon in the spiritual battle. This is quite a long psalm; try to read it thoughtfully and carefully, and go back over it during the week.

Prayer

Guard us, O Lord, with the shield of faith,
and fight for us with the sword of the Spirit,
that in all our spiritual warfare
against the powers of darkness
we may gain the victory
through Jesus Christ our Lord… Amen[12]

LINK-WORK

DAY TWO

Reading John 1:1–5; 8:12; and 12:28–36

John was particularly impressed with the themes of light and darkness. Read each of the three passages carefully and see what you learn about the power of Jesus' light.

Prayer

This is the last time in this course that you will be praying for your *Personal prayer need.* How has your prayer for this developed over the last five weeks? Thank God for where you have seen answered prayer. Decide whether you want to continue praying for this after the course, and if so, how and when.

LINK-WORK

DAY THREE

Reading Daniel 2:17–23 Daniel's prayer

This is a prayer of thanks which gives an insight into Daniel's prayer life. Daniel expresses confidence in God's control in the world, even though there was much going on that might have made Daniel believe otherwise. Daniel is able to give thanks to God in the midst of a crisis, because he looks to the character of God, rather than being fearful of the circumstances. It is also clear that Daniel was always open to receiving revelation during his prayer time. Spend some time today seeing how you can take these principles into your prayer life.

Prayer

Spend some moments in praise along the lines of Daniel's prayer. Fill in the gaps with the words that come to mind as you open your heart to God in praise:

Praise be to the name of God for ever and ever
He does...
He gives...
He reveals...
I thank and praise you O God of my fathers,
You have given me...
You have made known to me...

You may like to use the following prayer written by Lancelot Andrewes (died 1626):

Blessing and honour, and thanksgiving and praise,
  more than we can utter,
  more than we can conceive,
be unto thee, O holy and glorious Trinity,
  Father, Son and Holy Spirit,
by all angels, all people, all creatures,
  for ever and ever... Amen.

LINK-WORK

DAY FOUR

Reading for meditation Luke 22:31–32

Meditate on these verses today. Note the key thing here is that although we face temptation and are in the spiritual battle, our Lord Jesus is praying for us that we may not fail. *If God is for us, who can be against us...*

Prayer

The ancient Celtic church liked to do encompassing prayers as prayers of protection. Here is one you may like to use. As you pray it, you may like to follow their custom which is to extend your index finger and move it round clockwise around yourself. It draws an imaginary line around you with the good things of God within, and the evil things of darkness without.

Circle me, Lord
Keep protection near,
And danger afar.

Circle me, Lord
Keep hope within,
Keep doubt without.

Circle me, Lord
Keep light near,
And darkness afar.

Circle me, Lord
Keep peace within,
Keep evil out. ®

LINK-WORK

DAY FIVE

Reading Ephesians 1:15–23 Paul's prayer

This is a theologian praying! But Paul does not keep all his theology in his head or in books. He uses it powerfully in prayer for his friends. Spend a bit of time with this prayer today.

Prayer

We can all be theologians when nobody's looking! Try using this prayer today for a good friend. Where Paul uses "you", you can insert the name of your friend. Notice how good it feels to immerse this friend in such glorious truths. If you prefer, try writing a prayer for your friends in which you want to catch some of the great truths of our faith.

Today is the last time in this course that you will pray for your *Local prayer need.* As with the personal need, reflect on your prayers during the five weeks. Give thanks for answered prayer, and ask God whether he wants you to continue in prayer for this need.

LINK-WORK

DAY SIX

Reading Revelation 20:1–4 and 21:1–4

There are some puzzling bits in this reading, but focus today on the things which are abundantly clear. One day Jesus will return, he will once and for all destroy Satan and his demonic forces, he will abolish death, and there will be a new heaven and a new earth which knows nothing about sin and suffering. You have permission to get a bit excited about this!

Prayer

Thank God for the glorious hope we have of Jesus' return and all that means for this world.

Today is the last time to pray for your *Global prayer need*. As with the other two needs, reflect on your prayers during the five weeks. Give thanks for answered prayer, and ask God whether he wants you to continue in prayer for this need.

LINK-WORK

DAY SEVEN

Reading Psalm 100

This psalm (often known as the Jubilate) is a great psalm of thanks. Even when we are not in the mood to rejoice, it is good to have a discipline of giving thanks to God for all that he is. As you dwell on this psalm, allow the Spirit to stir thanksgiving in your heart.

The coming group meeting is the last of the course. During the meeting you will be asked to break into small groups and to identify three things that you have learned through this course. You might like to think about this now, and make a record in the space below:

Three things I have learned from this course:

1 _____

_____

2 _____

_____

3 _____

_____

Prayer

Give thanks to God today for leading you through this course and enabling you to be a Saint at Prayer! Pray for the coming meeting of your group.

PRAYER IDEA – PRAYER NET

In the Abbey on the island of Iona there has been a custom to have a prayer net. This is simply a net that is hanging from the wall and nearby there is a basket of short lengths of wool. People are invited to come near the net and offer a prayer for some particular need, and mark that prayer by attaching a piece of wool on the net. In time this net has become a colourful array, picturing the colour and strength of the prayers of God's people. You could have this same idea in your home, or in your church.

For the kingdom, the power and the glory are yours, now and for ever

Taking prayer out

TEACHING POINT

What is a prayer/listening walk?

In recent years the Spirit of God has been directing Christian people to move out of their churches and homes in care and concern for their neighbourhoods. This is evidenced in evangelism, social action and various prayer projects. God is stirring many people at this time to engage in *prayer walking*, and this is one excellent way of taking our prayer out into the streets. There is always a danger that a prayer meeting can become introverted and rather unconnected with the world around. The value of prayer walking is that it connects in a very real way our intercessory prayer life with the community around us.

The value of a *praise march* is that it is a very public witness for Christ for all to see. Not only this, but it is an opportunity for Christians to pray together for their neighbourhood.

The prayer/listening walk is also designed to take prayer on to the streets, but it is done privately. The purpose of this kind of walk is to listen and discern, and to then pray knowledgeably for the area according to what has been heard on the walk. The main emphasis for a prayer/listening walk is on the listening. The prayer part is keeping in touch with God, asking him to direct us and speak to us and reveal to us things we need to notice.

I am grateful to the Rev. Anne Long who has developed the concept of these listening walks in her work for Christian Listeners (a department of the Acorn Christian Healing Trust).

GUIDELINES

❖ **Be natural!** Look normal as you go along, and don't look like you are on a subversive mission!

❖ **Be sensitive to what is naturally around you.** This is a principle we were learning about earlier, to do with becoming aware of our surroundings. As you go along, ask the Spirit to awaken and alert you to seeing things that are in your community. The sort of things you might become aware of are…

Schools in your area – perhaps you never noticed that junior school before. How does the school look? Imagine what it feels like being a young child in this school.

Pubs – places where people meet together. Note the positives of friendships, relaxation, but also look out for the loneliness, the consequences of alcohol abuse.

Homes for the elderly – Imagine how it feels to live here. What is the architecture of the home saying? Is there a good feeling about this home?

Types of homes – small, large, well kept up, in need of repair. Houses and gardens say something about the people who live in them.

Shops – what kinds of things are sold here? Do they nourish people in mind and spirit as well as in body?

What is the **economy** of your area?

What is the **architecture** is saying – what did the town planners think about people when they designed this part of your town? Has that communicated good things or bad things to people's sense of self-worth?

How much **greenery** is there? Is there enough for people to be able to appreciate nature?

❖ **Give thanks for the positive things.** Where you see good things in your community, give quiet thanks and praise to God for the strong and good things he has give to your area. Bless what is good.

❖ **Be sensitive to what is spiritually around you.** We were giving attention last week to the spiritual battle and on the prayer walk you can be giving attention to this realm. Some people have an awareness of the spiritual 'atmosphere' of places. Be aware of the atmosphere as you walk. Does the region, or parts of it, have a sense of God's blessing and protection over it? If so, give thanks for it. Conversely, is there any sense of darkness over the place, brought about perhaps by human sin or sorrow either in the present or hanging over from the past?

To be sensitive in this area, you will need not only to be listening to what is naturally present, but also you will need to be open to the Holy Spirit prompting you about unseen spiritual realities. These things will be learned by inner promptings and discernment of spirits, and will need to be weighed and checked out with others.

Things here that you might be aware of…

Areas, buildings, homes which seem to you to be particularly strong spiritually. Where this is the case, thank God for blessing these places.

Areas, buildings or homes that feel to you to be somehow dark spiritually. Where this is the case, be asking God to reveal anything you need to know about the cause of that darkness, so that you might be able to pray accurately for it.

If you are familiar with the notion of territorial powers (sometimes called territorial spirits), that is evil forces that apparently occupy and oppress particular regions or territories, be alert to such influences. Listen carefully to God to see if you can hear why these powers were originally given rights in this particular region. For example, where a street has been for many years notorious for prostitution, then 'rights' have been granted to spirits of lust and exploitation, and these may well have become dark forces now oppressing people in the area.

Note: where such powers are discerned, and it is agreed in the group that they exist, then more specialist and persistent prayer will be required to shift them. It is not the kind of thing that beginners in spiritual warfare praying should engage in.

❖ **In general walk in silence.**

If necessary use your partner to check out your discernment of something, but don't let it become a conversation. Your main channels of communication are open to God and to the community.

Your primary task is listening, not interceding.

For anyone with an intercessor's heart, it will be quite a discipline not to get into intercessory prayer on this walk. Keep the intercession until you return to the group. On the walk, your praying is in asking God for guidance and revelation, and in thanking and praising him for the good things you have discovered in your neighbourhood.

❖ You might like to **make a note** of anything that particularly impressed you. Have a notepad and pen handy.

The gift of speaking in tongues

WHAT THE BIBLE SAYS

It is a gift of the Spirit

1 Corinthians 12:10

St Paul gives clear teaching about this gift that he calls *glossalalia* which literally translated means speaking in another language. In more poetic mood in 1 Corinthians 12:10 he refers to tongues of angels. It is therfore a heavenly language but can be used on earth.

It is a gift promised by Jesus

Mark 16:17

In this account of the commissioning of the disciples, Jesus says that speaking in tongues will be one of the signs accompanying the proclaimed word.

It is a language that we use to speak to God

1 Corinthians 14:2

Paul makes clear that this gift is a language of the spirit addressed to God. We won't always have an understanding of this language. When someone speaks in tongues he *utters mysteries with his spirit* (1 Corinthians 14:2) It is not a language of the mind, but it is subject to our will. We can speak in tongues at will. We use it to worship God, or for intercessory prayer to him. When we pray in tongues we pray *with the spirit* (1 Corinthians 14:14–15). One of the great benefits of the gift of tongues is that it frees our spirits to communicate with God without the complication of the mind having to understand it, and find conventional words to express things which are often beyond words. Private tongues does not require interpretation. Tongues can also be used very effectively corporately either in worship (sung) or in intercession (usually said). When used in this way it does not require interpretation.

It is self-edifying

1 Corinthians 14:4

When we use tongues it builds us up. It is the one gift that can be used to encourage ourselves. But our speaking in tongues won't build others up unless it is interpreted. Paul clearly often spoke in tongues, but note his warning, *I would rather speak five intelligible words to instruct others than ten thousand words in a tongue* (1 Corinthians14:19).

Interpreting 1 Corinthians 12:10 and 14:27–28

Sometimes in a meeting, someone feels moved to pray out loud in a tongue. Everyone should listen to this, and someone will be given a gift of interpretation, which might sound similar to a prophecy.

It often accompanies baptism of the Holy Spirit Acts 2:4

When the disciples were baptised in the Spirit at Pentecost they all experienced this gift. Often when people receive this experience they speak in tongues as well. See also Acts 19:1–7: when Paul laid his hands on the heads of the Ephesian believers *the Holy Spirit came upon them and they spoke in tongues and prophesied.*

APPENDIX TWO
Sources

Prayer by Richard Foster, Hodder and Stoughton, 1992

❶ page 195
❸ pages 205–206 (read pages 203–206 if you want to study this further)
❺ pages 197–199

❷ From *The Prayer Book of the Episcopal Church of the USA*

By Stony Paths by Jim Cotter, Cairns Publications, 1991

❹ page 17–18

Fern Seeds and Elephants by C. S. Lewis, Collins, 1975

❻ page 40

Celebrating Common Prayer by Mowbray, 1992

❼ page 557
⓬ page 516

Iona Community Worship Book by Wild Goose Publications, 1991

❽ page 73

Commentary on Matthew Volume I by William Barclay, St Andrew Press, 1975

❾ page 225

Quoted in *Celtic Fire* by Robert Van de Weyer, DLT, 1990

❿ page 55

⓫ For further reading about this subject, see *Those Tiresome Intruders* by Graham Dow, Grove Pastoral Series No. 41

The Edge of Glory by David Adam, Triangle, 1985

⓭ page 8

Other books from Anglican Renewal Ministries

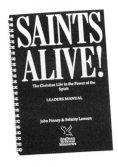

Saints in Evangelism
J. John

A superb training course in 'friendship evangelism' created by J. John. Designed for small groups, there are six sessions, with workbooks for members and a video to guide you through the course. (240-minute video—6 x 30 minutes.)

Workbook, £2.99; Video, £25 inc. VAT

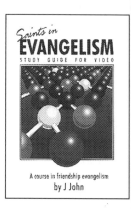

Saints Alive!
John Finney and Felicity Lawson

Already used by more than 100,000 people, this is a nine-week course on the basics of Christian discipleship. It is suitable for for new Christians and confirmation, as well as for churches learning about renewal.

Workbook, £1.99; Leaders Manual, £5.99; Video, £15 inc. VAT

Saints for Healing
Roger Vaughan

A nine-week course for groups making their first steps in the healing ministry.

Workbook, £1.99; Leader's Manual, £5.99

Saints in Worship
Derek Howell

A nine-week course exploring the theory and practice of worship.

Pack: Leader's Manual, one sample workbook and two cassettes, £20 inc. VAT. Additional workbooks, £2.99

Young Saints
Alan Price

A unique concept in mid-week 'housegroups for 8–11 year-olds'—successfully pioneered by Captain Alan Price of the Church Army. Ideal as a course for confirmation preparation.

The pack includes six weeks' material (plus optional two weeks' on confirmation) with magazine-style worksheets, detailed resources for the leader, pens, badges, etc.

Children's Pack, £5; Leader's Pack, £15; Additional Leader's Book, £9.99. (Prices inc. VAT)

▲ Lynx Communications ORDER FORM

Title	ISBN	Price	Qty	Total
Anglican Renewal Ministries				
Saints in Evangelism				
Video Guide	3147 2	£25*	......	......
Workbook	3146 4	£2.99	......	......
Saints Alive!				
Leader's Manual	3141 3	£5.99	......	......
Video	3142 1	£15*	......	......
Workbook	3140 5	£1.99	......	......
Saints for Healing				
Leader's Manual	3145 6	£5.99	......	......
Workbook	3144 8	£1.99	......	......
Saints in Worship				
Leader's Pack	3151 0	£20*	......	......
Additional Leader's Books	3150 2	£9.99	......	......
Workbooks	3149 9	£2.99	......	......
Young Saints				
Children's Pack	3154 5	£5*	......	......
Leader's Pack	3155 3	£15*	......	......
Additional Leader's Books	3156 1	£9.99	......	

* price includes VAT

Total Value: £ ....

All available through Christian bookshops, or post or phone your order direct to:

**LYNX COMMUNICATIONS
Peter's Way, Sandy Lane West
OXFORD OX4 5HG Tel: 0865 747550**

POSTAGE AND PACKING

Up to £50 order value: UK, add £2.50;
Rest of the world, add £3.50.
From £50 to £100:   UK, add £5;
Rest of the world, add £7.
More than £100:   Postage and packing free.

PAYMENT

I enclose a cheque made payable to Lynx Communications for

£..

Please debit my Access/Visa/Mastercard/Eurocard account no.

Card expiry date...................................

Signature...

Please deliver to:

Name ....

Address ....

....

....

Postcode ....

Tel ....

Please keep me informed about new LYNX publications in the following areas:

Computer software:

PC	☐
CD-ROM	☐

Training resources:

Evangelism	☐
Youth Work	☐
Pastoral Care	☐
Social Action	☐
Christian Doctrine	☐

Other: ....

BIBLE READING FELLOWSHIP Our partner publisher, Bible Reading Fellowship, produces Bible reading notes and resource books for groups and individuals. If you would like details of their publications, please tick here: ☐

Data Protection Act: If you do not wish us to keep a record of your name for the purpose of sending information on future LYNX publications, tick here: ☐

Notes

Notes

Notes